Blizzards

Blizzards

Patrick Merrick

THE CHILD'S WORLD®, INC.

Library of Congress Cataloging-in-Publication Data
Merrick, Patrick.
Blizzards / by Patrick Merrick.
p. cm.
Includes index.
Summary: Uses a question-and-answer format to provide
information about the causes of blizzards, where they occur,
their characteristics, and the effects they produce.
ISBN 1-56766-469-5 (lib. bdg. : alk paper)
1. Blizzards—Miscellanea—Juvenile literature.
[1. Blizzards—Miscellanea. 2. Questions and answers.] I. Title
QC926.37.M47 1998
551.55′5—dc21   97-28754
CIP
AC

Photo Credits

© 1993 Cindy Jones/Dembinsky Photo Assoc. Inc.: 23
© Clyde H. Smith/Tony Stone Images: 29
© Daniel J. Cox/Tony Stone Images: cover
© Donovan Reese/Tony Stone Images: 19, 20
© Frank Oberle/Tony Stone Images: 24
© Jake Evans/Tony Stone Images: 9
© 1997 John Mielcarek/Dembinsky Photo Assoc. Inc.: 16
© 1997 John S. Botkin/Dembinsky Photo Assoc. Inc.: 15
© 1993 Ken Scott/Dembinsky Photo Assoc. Inc.: 30
© Richard H. Smith/Tony Stone Images: 26
© Stewart Cohen/Tony Stone Images: 2
© Stuart Cohen/Comstock, Inc.: 6
© Stuart Westmorland/Tony Stone Images: 10
© 1996 Willard Clay/Dembinsky Photo Assoc. Inc.: 13

On the cover...

Front cover: These trees are hard to see during a blizzard.
Page 2: This man is walking during the beginning of a blizzard.

Table of Contents

What Is a Blizzard?

The wind blows gently on a cold winter day. As the sky turns cloudy, snow begins to fall. Throughout the day, the snow falls faster and faster. The wind is now blowing so hard that you find it difficult to see. What started as a soft snowfall has turned into a fierce storm. It is a blizzard!

⇐ Sometimes big snowflakes fall during a blizzard.

Not all snowstorms are blizzards. But blizzards are the most dangerous type of winter storm. That is because blizzards mix snow with terrible winds and very cold temperatures. The winds blow faster than 35 miles an hour. That often makes temperatures feel like 20 degrees below zero—or even colder!

It is easy to see how hard winds can blow during a blizzard. ⇒

Where Do Blizzards Happen?

If you live somewhere that has snow, you have probably seen a blizzard. Northern Europe, Canada, Russia, and the northern United States have the most blizzards. People who live in these places see about five blizzards each year.

Most blizzards happen during December, January, and February. Sometimes, though, they occur as early as October or as late as May. In fact, the biggest snowfall in the U.S. happened during April. In April of 1921, 76 inches of snow fell in Silver Lake, Colorado, in just one day!

⇐ A blizzard has just passed through this forest in Oregon.

What Causes Blizzards?

Water and sunlight are needed to make a blizzard. As the sun warms Earth's oceans, lakes, and rivers, the air above the water rises. As it rises, it carries drops of water with it. This movement is called **evaporation**. The air and water keep rising until they are high in the sky. But the temperature up there is cold! It is so cold that the water turns into tiny pieces of ice called **crystals**.

Water from this mountain stream is slowly evaporating. ⇒

In the sky, billions of ice crystals come together inside huge clouds. As the crystals mix together, they get bigger and bigger. Finally, they **condense**, or become too heavy to stay in the clouds. When this happens, the crystals fall to the earth. If the temperature near the ground is warm, the crystals melt and form rain. If the temperature is cold, the crystals stay frozen and form snow. We often call falling ice crystals *snowflakes*.

These clouds are full of ice crystals. ⇒

How Dangerous Are Blizzards?

Blizzards kill hundreds of people every year. They also cause millions of dollars' worth of damage. Heavy snow can block roads and keep ambulances and police from getting to people who need help. The weight of the snow can cause buildings to cave in. Power lines can snap from the snow and ice, leaving people trapped in their homes without phones or electricity.

⇐ These power lines are covered with ice after a blizzard.

A blizzard's high winds are very dangerous. They blow the snow around and make it very hard to see. Sometimes, people who are caught outside during a blizzard get lost. They travel in circles for hours trying to find a safe place to wait out the storm.

The car in this photo is having a hard time traveling in a blizzard. ⇒

The most dangerous part of a blizzard, though, is the cold. When the wind blows fast, the air feels even colder than it really is. This is called the **windchill**.

People exposed to very cold windchills lose their body heat very fast. Sometimes a part of the body gets so cold that it freezes. This is called **frostbite**. Frostbite happens most often to ears, faces, fingers, or toes. When a person's whole body loses heat, that is called **hypothermia**. Hypothermia is a very serious condition. The person becomes sleepy and can even freeze to death.

Can Blizzards Cause Other Disasters?

Even when a blizzard is over, it can still cause disasters. Sometimes a large amount of snow falls off a mountain. The snow tumbles and rumbles down, burying trees and anything in its way. This kind of disaster is called an **avalanche**. Avalanches cause a lot of damage and can hurt many people.

This avalanche in Switzerland is creating a white cloud of snow. ⇒

Blizzards can also cause floods. When spring comes, the snow from all the blizzards melts. If there has been too much snow, the rivers and lakes cannot hold all the water. The water spreads out in a flood, damaging towns and farms.

What Should You Do in a Blizzard?

If you are ever caught in a blizzard, the best thing to do is stay inside! Television and radio stations can warn you about blizzards in plenty of time. If you must go outside, wear several layers of clothes. Make sure your head, feet, face, and hands are well covered.

If you are ever trapped in a car during a blizzard, stay with the car! It is a good idea to make an emergency pack and put it in the car before winter begins. That way, it is there when you need it. The pack should have extra blankets, a shovel, a flashlight, batteries, and high-energy foods like candy. These things will help you stay alive until help comes.

This person is staying in his car during a blizzard. ⇒

The winter is a wonderful time to be outdoors. When it snows, it is fun to go skiing, hiking, sledding, or just playing in the snow. But if the sky gets dark and the wind begins to blow, it is time to go inside. That way, you will stay safe from the dangerous winter storm—the blizzard.

Glossary

avalanche (A–vuh–lanch)
An avalanche occurs when snow breaks loose and slides down a mountain.

crystals (KRIH-stulz)
Crystals are pieces of ice that form very high in the sky. Clouds are full of ice crystals.

condense (kuhn–DENS)
When something condenses, it gets smaller and heavier. When ice crystals condense, they fall to earth as either snow or rain.

evaporation (ee–vah–puh–RAY–shun)
When water rises into the air, it is called evaporation.

frostbite (FROST BITE)
Frostbite is frozen skin caused by very cold temperatures.

hypothermia (hy-poh–THER–mee–uh)
Hypothermia is a drop in a person's whole body temperature. Hypothermia can be very dangerous.

windchill (WIND–chill)
Windchill is how cold the air feels. Blowing wind makes the air feel colder than it really is.

Index